NATIONAL MONUMENTS EVENTS AND TIMES

by **Jeff Putnam**

National Monuments: Events and Times
by Jeff Putnam

Photography: p.2 ©CORBIS; p.4 ©Reuters NewMedia Inc./CORBIS; p.6 ©Paul A. Souders/CORBIS; p.8 ©Underwood & Underwood/CORBIS; p.10 ©Bettmann/CORBIS; p.12 ©Lee Snider; Lee Snider/CORBIS; p.13 ©David Muench/CORBIS; p.14 ©Dave G. Houser/CORBIS; p.18 ©Joseph Sohm; Visions of America/CORBIS; p.20 ©Bettmann/CORBIS; p.21 ©Paul A. Souders/CORBIS; p.23 ©William A. Bake/CORBIS; p.25 ©Tria Giovan/CORBIS; p.27 ©Bettmann/CORBIS; p.29 ©Minnesota Historical Society/CORBIS; p.31 ©Catherine Karnow/CORBIS; p.32 ©CORBIS; p.35 ©R. Morley/PhotoLink/Getty Images; p.38 ©Wolfgang Kaehler/CORBIS; p.40 ©CORBIS; p.42 ©James P. Blair/CORBIS; p.46 ©Hulton-Deutsch Collection/CORBIS; p.48 top ©Lee Snider; Lee Snider/CORBIS; p.48 bottom ©Bettmann/CORBIS; p.50 ©Bettmann/CORBIS; p.52 ©Bettmann/CORBIS; p.54 ©Bettmann/CORBIS; p.55 ©Bettmann/CORBIS; p.58 left ©Underwood & Underwood/CORBIS; p.58 right ©Bettmann/CORBIS; p.60 ©Bettmann/CORBIS; p.61 ©Leonard de Selva/CORBIS; p.63 ©G.E. Kidder Smith/CORBIS; p.65 ©Mark E. Gibson/CORBIS; p.67 ©D. Falconer/PhotoLink/Getty Images; p.69 ©Bettmann/CORBIS

Nonfiction Reviewer
John Barell, Ed.D.
Educational Consultant, The American Museum of Natural History
New York City

Design, Production, and Art Buying by
Inkwell Publishing Solutions, Inc., New York City
Cover Design by
Inkwell Publishing Solutions, Inc., New York City

ISBN: 0-7367-1787-0
Copyright © Zaner-Bloser, Inc.

All rights reserved. No part of this book may be reproduced or transmitted in any form or by any means, electronic or mechanical, including photocopying, recording, or by any information storage and retrieval system, without permission in writing from the Publisher.

Web sites have been carefully researched for accuracy, content, and appropriateness. However, Web sites are subject to change. Internet usage should always be monitored.

Zaner-Bloser, Inc., P.O. Box 16764, Columbus, Ohio 43216-6764, 1-800-421-3018

Printed in China

03   04   05   06   07   (321)   5   4   3   2   1

TABLE OF CONTENTS

Introduction
National Monuments 1

Chapter 1
The Great Stone Faces 6

Chapter 2
The Birth of America 11

Chapter 3
The New Nation Spreads Its Wings 16

Chapter 4
Tested by War 22

Chapter 5
A Birthday Present 32

Chapter 6
Wars in Recent Times 37

Chapter 7
Struggling for Justice 45

Chapter 8
Celebrating America's Greatness 57

Chapter 9
Fire and Water 66

Bibliography 72

Glossary 73

Index 74

INTRODUCTION
NATIONAL MONUMENTS

What do you think of when you hear the words *national monument*? Some people think of the Statue of Liberty. Others think of the Lincoln Memorial or the battlefield at Gettysburg. National monuments are important landmarks, structures, and historic sites. The national government has set them aside for people to study and enjoy.

The United States has more than seventy national monuments. They fall into three main categories: monuments to important people, monuments to wonders of nature, and monuments to important events and times.

Outstanding People

Many of our most famous national monuments honor great Americans. Maybe you have visited Washington, D.C. There, the towering Washington Monument honors our first president, George Washington. The mighty Lincoln Memorial celebrates President Abraham Lincoln. A statue of Thomas Jefferson, our third president, stands watch in the Jefferson Memorial. Have you seen any of these monuments? You honor the achievements of these leaders when you visit their memorials.

Famous Americans are also honored in other ways. Their birthplaces, homes, and workplaces have become national monuments, too. For example, you can walk through the house where Henry Wadsworth Longfellow wrote his poetry. The laboratory where Thomas Edison built many of his famous inventions is waiting for your visit. You can stroll across the battlefields where George Washington led the Continental Army.

Wonders of Nature

Other national monuments are sites of great natural beauty. They include smoking volcanoes, weird rock formations, breathtaking vistas, unusual trees, and untouched wilderness.

Thomas Edison

Some monuments allow you to explore a cave, swim in a coral reef, or trudge up a sand dune. You can also paddle through a swamp or look for ancient fossils. Do you like to hike? You can take a 2,100-mile (3,380-km) hike on a trail that passes through 14 states, the Appalachian Trail. The government set aside and protected this trail for everyone to enjoy.

Events and Times to Remember

This third category of national monuments is the one you'll read about in this book. Many of our monuments honor important events in our nation's history. Did you know that you can walk on the beach where the first airplane flew? Or sit in the room where the women's rights movement actually began?

You can explore the places where important battles were fought, scientific discoveries were made, and historic documents were signed. Imagine what it would be like to stand where the Civil War began or where our freedom from Great Britain was finally won.

Would you like to see the place where our national anthem was inspired? You can also explore where the Constitution was written and the Declaration of Independence was signed. You can see where railroads and canals first began to reach across the country. You can stand where the first European explorers of America stood. You can even visit the homes of people who lived in our country thousands of years before the Europeans arrived.

Some of our national monuments help us remember sad times and events. For example, the Oklahoma City National Memorial honors and remembers the 168 people who were killed by a terrorist bombing. Other monuments remind us of terrible acts committed in the past. You can see where many Native Americans lost their lives. You can explore prison camps where Japanese Americans were forced to live during World War II.

Oklahoma City National Memorial

Washington, D.C., is the site of a monument to the nation's most controversial war. On it, you can read the names of those who died in Vietnam. At these national monuments, Americans can remember both the good and the not so good in their country's history.

Pride in Our Country

Are any national monuments near where you live? Have you visited one of them? America's history, heritage, and natural beauty are preserved in its national monuments. That way, you, other Americans, and people from around the world can experience them. Future generations will be able to enjoy them, too. These national monuments help us take pride in America. They also teach us about the past. Learning about our past can help us prepare for an even brighter future.

In this book, you will learn about many important events that helped shape our country. You will read about the special places that everyone can visit, places that make these historical events live again!

Which of these monuments would you like to see?

CHAPTER 1
The Great Stone Faces

Can you name the four famous faces on Mount Rushmore? They are Presidents George Washington, Thomas Jefferson, Theodore Roosevelt, and Abraham Lincoln. Mount Rushmore National Monument honors these great presidents and the important events in our history that they influenced.

Can you name the person responsible for creating Mount Rushmore? Probably not. It belongs to an almost unknown man. He worked for 14 years to make his dream a reality. This monument also honors him. His name was Gutzon Borglum. Long before he began Mount Rushmore,

Borglum had admired ancient stone carvings in Egypt and the Middle East. After working on other large sculptures, he turned his attention to a certain mountain in the Black Hills of South Dakota. Why did he select this site, so far away from everything? He had good reasons: The southeast side of Mount Rushmore is smooth, light-colored granite. It also receives sunlight all year long.

At first, Borglum thought the mountainside would have room for only three presidents. George Washington would represent independence and liberty. Thomas Jefferson would stand for self-government and democracy. Abraham Lincoln would represent the permanence of our union.

However, Borglum soon found that the mountainside had room for another face. Whom should he choose? After much thought, he selected Theodore Roosevelt. This president was chosen for his important role in world affairs.

Which president would you have chosen to be the fourth face? Why?

Borglum assembled his team of stone carvers, miners, loggers, and others. Work started in 1927. The first step was making models of the heads. At the foot of Mount Rushmore, Borglum made a smaller, rougher version of each head. The models were one-twelfth the size of the finished carvings. Borglum used a measuring system called *pointing*. It helped him make sure the large carvings on the mountain matched the smaller models. This system involved locating points on the nose, mouth, and eyes of the models. These points were then matched on the larger faces.

However, in 1928, work stopped. The money that people had contributed had been spent. Fortunately, the next year Congress voted to give $250,000 to Borglum's project. The team was able to start working again. Later that same year, however, the Great Depression began. The stock market crashed, and money dried up again. Many people began to doubt that the massive project

Workers using powerful tools to create Jefferson

would ever be completed. Can you imagine how Borglum felt as he faced so many problems?

Little work was done over the next few years. However, in 1934, Congress again funded the project. Finally, Gutzon Borglum's dream would come true.

While Borglum supervised, his team of workers carved the giant faces out of solid rock. They began by dynamiting large chunks of rock out of the mountainside. Then they created special leather seats that allowed them to hang over the edge of the cliff. In these seats, dangling high in the air, they drilled, chipped, and chiseled away the rock.

Powerful air hammers made the job a little easier. Slowly, the faces of the four presidents began to emerge from the granite. From the valley below, Gutzon Borglum studied the emerging faces. He checked them from different angles and in different light.

For seven more years, the team battled weather, money problems, and the hard granite of Mount Rushmore. By 1941, the end of this awesome task was near. The carvers had removed 450,000 tons of rock. The faces were 60 feet (18 m) high. Sadly, the man who had designed and supervised the carving did not live to see it completed. Gutzon Borglum died in 1941. His son Lincoln finished the project.

DID YOU KNOW?

Mount Rushmore

- The noses on the heads are 20 feet (6 m) long.
- South Dakota officials at first wanted Gutzon Borglum to show Wild West heroes. The sculptor convinced them to choose great American presidents instead.
- You can see the heads in a scene from an Alfred Hitchcock movie. Actor Cary Grant escapes from villains by climbing down the sculptures.

Repairing Abraham Lincoln's nose, Mount Rushmore, South Dakota

Today, Presidents Washington, Jefferson, Roosevelt, and Lincoln, beam proudly at visitors. Looking at them, you'll be reminded of the important events connected with each man. George Washington led our young nation to victory over the British and served as our first president. Thomas Jefferson guided the nation as it began to spread westward over the continent. Abraham Lincoln preserved the country when the Civil War threatened to snuff out the candle of unity. Theodore Roosevelt reminded the nation of the need to protect its natural beauty and resources.

If you go to Mount Rushmore, you can learn more about this world-famous monument. You can marvel at the dedication and courage of the people who created the sculptures, especially Gutzon Borglum.

CHAPTER 2
THE BIRTH OF AMERICA

Many of our national monuments honor the Revolutionary War. They help us remember the important events of the war, from the first shot to the last surrender.

The Shot Heard 'Round the World

The first shots of the War of Independence were fired in Massachusetts in April 1775. Paul Revere and others had spread the warning that the British army was marching on the village of Concord. There the patriots had stored weapons, ammunition, and other supplies. A band of minutemen had gathered on the nearby Lexington Green. They had promised to be ready to fight "in a minute." Can you picture how nervous these men must have been as the redcoats marched by on their way to Concord?

Then a shot rang out and a battle began. Soon eight minutemen were dead and ten others were wounded. As the battle continued, redcoats fell. The war for American independence had begun.

Today, Lexington and Concord are part of Minute Man National Historical Park. A bridge over the Concord River is guarded by a famous statue of a minuteman. It was created by Daniel Chester French.

The Darkest Hour

At Valley Forge, in eastern Pennsylvania, General George Washington and 12,000 cold and hungry troops from the Continental Army spent the bitter winter of 1777–1778. Here is how Washington himself described the men's suffering:

To see men without clothes . . . without blankets . . . without shoes . . . without a house or hut . . . is a proof of patience and obedience which, in my opinion, can scarcely be paralleled.

Can you imagine the courage and faith of the Continental Army? Instead of giving up, the soldiers survived the bitterly cold winter. They trained and regained their strength. By the time spring finally arrived, the army had become a powerful, united fighting force. With new spirit, they were able to continue the war.

Minuteman statue at Concord

If you visit Valley Forge, you can see the small stone house where Washington had his headquarters. You can explore places where cannons were stored, where soldiers lived, and where **barricades** were built. Most of all, you can learn how the courage of the soldiers and their commander kept alive the dream of liberty. Its flame did not go out, even during the brutal winter at Valley Forge.

The Turning Point

At the war's start, most people gave the colonists little chance of defeating the mighty British. In fact, for the first two years, the colonists had few successes.

The experienced British generals had a plan to win the war. They would divide the colonies along New York's Hudson River. That would separate the New England colonies from the rest. In spring 1777, the redcoats, under General John Burgoyne, marched south from Canada towards New York City. They expected to be joined by British troops coming from the east. Together, they would trap the colonists.

Saratoga National Historical Park, New York

However, colonial soldiers stopped the troops coming from the east. When Burgoyne attacked the Continental Army, he met fierce resistance. The colonists gradually forced the British to retreat to the town of Saratoga, New York. There, the British were surrounded. Finally, on October 17, Burgoyne surrendered.

The ragtag colonists had defeated the mighty British army! They must have been joyous, don't you think? This victory helped determine the outcome of the war, partly because it impressed the French. They decided to help the colonists in their fight for independence.

British rampart at Saratoga National Historical Park

Today, you can visit the battlefields around Saratoga in upstate New York. They have been preserved as the Saratoga National Historical Park. They help us remember this crucial event in our nation's history.

Birth of a Nation

The dream of the soldiers at Lexington, Concord, Valley Forge, and Saratoga came true almost four years later. It happened at a place not far from George Washington's birthplace in eastern Virginia.

With the help of French allies, Washington's Continental Army had trapped a large British force. They were pinned down on a narrow piece of land near Yorktown. Washington's cannons blasted the British positions for nine days. The French fleet made it impossible for the British to escape by sea. On October 17, 1781, British Commander Lord Cornwallis asked to surrender.

The British still controlled several major cities. Nevertheless, the war was over. The British people no longer had the heart to support the war. In 1783, a peace **treaty** was signed, and the United States was born.

The Yorktown battlefield is part of the Colonial National Historical Park. One section of this park tells the story of Yorktown and the winning of American independence. The other section focuses on Jamestown, the first permanent English settlement in North America.

Visitors to the park can see where the English dream of a new colony was born. They can also see where it died.

CHAPTER 3
THE NEW NATION SPREADS ITS WINGS

During the twenty years after the Revolutionary War, the young country added a few new states and territories to the original thirteen. Then in 1803, the nation took a giant step forward. This giant step is remembered by a stunning national monument in St. Louis, Missouri.

The Jefferson National Expansion Memorial in St. Louis is the world's highest freestanding arch. It honors the beginning of the westward movement in America. It is named for Thomas Jefferson, who encouraged people to move to the West.

Into the Unknown

Did you ever buy something without knowing much about it? In 1803, President Jefferson took this risk, in a very big way. He decided to buy the vast area of plains, forests, and mountains known as the Louisiana Territory. It had belonged to France. The region stretched from the Mississippi River to the Rocky Mountains and from the Canadian border to Texas. Its 827,000 square miles (2,141,000 sq km) doubled the size of the young country.

Jefferson, like most Americans, had no idea what this land was like. Who lived there? Did it contain valuable natural resources? What plants grew there? What animals roamed the region?

In 1804, Jefferson sent Meriwether Lewis and William Clark to explore the Louisiana Territory. Their two-year journey took them all the way to the Pacific Ocean. They returned with information about the land and its plants and animals. Lewis and Clark made contact with different groups of Native Americans living there. They drew maps, crossed mountains, and rafted rivers. Thanks to their courage, the United States learned much about its new territory.

Lewis and Clark had begun their trip in St. Louis. At the time, it was a small town near where the Mississippi and Missouri Rivers meet. Thousands of other pioneers and settlers also used the city as their jumping-off point. Through much of the 1800s, St. Louis was the business center of the West, a true gateway. Settlers bought their supplies in the city. Merchants shipped their products through the town's Mississippi River port. Later, railroads passed through St. Louis as they crossed the nation. It must have been a very busy place, don't you think?

Today, the soaring steel arch symbolizes the city's role as a gateway and the movement of settlers to the West. Designed by Finnish American architect Eero Saarinen, the Gateway Arch rises 630 feet (192 m) into the air. It contains no supporting frame. Only its steel skin and its hollow triangular legs hold it up. You might think this would make the arch weak and shaky, but it doesn't. In fact, small cars inside the arch will take you to an observation area at the top. There, you'll be rewarded with a breathtaking view of the city and the river far below.

Jefferson National Expansion Memorial

Beneath the arch is an underground museum, the Museum of Westward Expansion. The arch, the museum, and the city's Old Courthouse are all part of the Jefferson National Expansion Memorial. The site honors the spirit of exploration, the bravery of the pioneers, and the wisdom of the president who made westward expansion possible.

A Winter Home

Another site also celebrates the famous journey of Meriwether Lewis and William Clark. It's Fort Clatsop National Monument. This small wooden fort is in a deep, dark Oregon forest near the Pacific Ocean. Here, the explorers spent the winter of 1806. They had just finished a dangerous journey of 4,000 miles that took 19 months.

On the way, they had hired a French fur trader named Toussaint Charbonneau. He was a guide and interpreter. Charbonneau's wife was a Shoshone named Sacagawea. (Does her name sound familiar to you? Her image is on the dollar coin.) Sacagawea served as a translator when Lewis and Clark met other Native Americans during the trip.

Charbonneau, Sacagawea, and their baby also spent the winter at Fort Clatsop. On March 23, 1806, the explorers set out on their return trip to St. Louis. When they arrived six months later, they were greeted as heroes. Their journey became famous.

Today, people easily travel between St. Louis and Oregon. Think about how different the journey must have been when Lewis and Clark made it!

By the Dawn's Early Light

Shortly after Lewis and Clark returned to St. Louis, another event took place that helped shape our country's destiny. The year was 1814. The United States was fighting the War of 1812 against Great Britain. Many Americans feared that they might lose their hard-won independence. They might once again become British colonies.

In the summer of 1814, British troops burned parts of Washington, D.C. In September, Britain began to focus on the important port of Baltimore, Maryland. Its powerful navy sailed north to attack Baltimore; only Fort McHenry protected the city from the might of the British navy. On September 13, the British attacked.

Illustration of the American flag still waving

A young American lawyer watched and waited through the all-night attack. He feared the fort would fall to the fierce bombardment. If you had waited there with him, what would you have talked about during those long hours?

When dawn broke, however, the man saw the broad stripes and bright stars of his nation's flag. They still waved over the fort. It was then that the young man, Francis Scott Key, knew that the British attack had failed.

In his happiness, Key quickly wrote down the first lines of a poem. Later, he finished the poem. He called it "Defense of Fort McHenry." It was published in a local newspaper and became an instant hit. Later, the poem was

Fort McHenry National Monument

set to music. The song became known by the name Key gave to the flag. In 1931, "The Star-Spangled Banner" was officially chosen as our national anthem.

If you visit Fort McHenry National Monument today, you can see the walls of the old star-shaped fort. You can walk through exhibits about the fort, the battle, and the young lawyer who wrote the famous poem.

You'll see something else, too. It is 42 feet (13 m) long and 30 feet (9 m) wide. Still waving over Fort McHenry is the star-spangled banner. It looks just like the flag that lifted the spirits of Francis Scott Key on that morning long ago. Next time you listen to "The Star-Spangled Banner" think how Key must have felt.

CHAPTER 4
TESTED BY WAR

America's national monuments tell of more than 200 years of war and peace, good times and hard times. Many people and events have created this long, proud history.

No event had a greater effect on our nation than the Civil War. Northerners battled Southerners. Brother fought brother. Can you imagine how families were torn apart? The issues were slavery and the preservation of the Union. More than 530,000 Americans from both sides died. Another 280,000 Union soldiers and an unknown number of Confederates were wounded. Civilians also suffered, and the destruction of property was immense.

The Civil War will probably remain as the most powerful event in our history, no matter how long the country endures. Today at our national monuments, you can see where the war began. You can also see where it was fought and where it finally ended.

It Begins

The place where the first shots of this terrible war were fired is now calm and peaceful. However, in the spring of 1861, tensions between the Northern and Southern states were growing. Southerners feared the new president, Abraham Lincoln. They were afraid he would try to destroy slavery. The Southern way of life depended on slavery continuing. South Carolina became the first state

Fort Sumter National Historic Site

to **secede** from, or leave, the United States. It was soon joined by ten other Southern states. Together, they formed the Confederate States of America.

In April, all Southern eyes turned toward a small island in the harbor of Charleston, South Carolina. On the island was Fort Sumter. This federal fort was defended by 85 soldiers under the command of Major Robert Anderson. Jefferson Davis, the new president of the Confederacy, demanded that federal troops leave Fort Sumter. When President Lincoln refused to move them, the Confederate soldiers opened fire.

The battle began at 4:30 on the morning of April 12, 1861. Confederate cannonballs and mortar shells rained down on Fort Sumter. The bombardment was intense, but Major Anderson refused to surrender the fort. The Confederates continued their attack on April 13. Suddenly, red-hot cannonballs crashed into the officers' **barracks** in the fort. They set it ablaze. The fire quickly spread to other parts of Fort Sumter. It created thick smoke and extreme heat. Then the fire crept dangerously close to a gunpowder storage area. The Union defenders had a difficult choice to make: surrender or continue fighting and risk total destruction. What would you have done?

By late afternoon, after 34 hours of bombardment, Anderson made his decision. His men could no longer hold out against the Confederate cannons. Fort Sumter surrendered. The federal troops sailed for the North the next day. Do you think they knew they had fired the first shots in the nation's most terrible war?

Almost exactly four years later on April 14, 1865, Major Robert Anderson returned to Charleston. The war was over, and the Union had been restored. Anderson himself raised the flag over Fort Sumter. It was the same flag he had lowered four years earlier. Can you imagine the different feelings he had?

Today, Fort Sumter is a National Historic Site. It contains a museum and exhibits. Visitors can walk along the walls and see the scars from the first battle of the Civil War.

The following four long years of fighting tested the nation's spirit like no other challenge, before or since.

Civil War artifacts

The names of the greatest battles of the Civil War are legendary. You probably know many of them. How would it feel to walk on the battlefields of Gettysburg, Bull Run, Antietam, or Shiloh? You'd probably want to know more about the thousands of men who fought there. What were their thoughts as they marched out to meet the enemy? Were they afraid? Did they carry pictures of their loved ones and letters from home?

The first large battle of the war took place near the village of Manassas in Virginia. That's just west of Washington, D.C. In July 1861, federal troops marched out to explore the Virginia countryside. They met a large force of Confederate troops.

Most Northerners expected this battle—and the war—to be won quickly. In fact, many people, including Congressmen and their families, had followed the Union Army to watch the "Rebels" be crushed.

However, the Confederates had other plans. They spoiled the Union's idea and soundly defeated the overconfident federal troops. The federal troops went scurrying back to the safety of Washington. They were followed closely by the **civilians** who had come to watch the battle as if it were a play. The North suffered a crushing defeat at Manassas, also known as Bull Run. Afterward, the North knew it was in for a long, terrible war against a worthy foe. Today, you can explore Manassas, a national battlefield park. You might try to imagine where the civilians stood to watch the battle.

The War Rages On

Following Manassas, the armies battled all across the South. One site preserved today is Shiloh in southwestern Tennessee. It was the first major battle in the West. In April 1862, Union forces invaded Tennessee and Mississippi, trying to gain control of the rivers. They were met by Confederate forces, and a bitter battle followed. The slaughter was incredible. One part of the battle became known as the "Hornet's Nest." Why this name?— the number of bullets flying through the air reminded the soldiers of hornets!

After much terrible fighting, the Union forces were able to defeat the Confederates. The victorious Union commander would be heard from again, as would his

The battle at Shiloh

brilliant assistant. You may have heard of them, too. They were Ulysses S. Grant and William Tecumseh Sherman. You can learn more about these men and the battle they fought at Shiloh National Military Park.

   A key battle of the early Civil War is remembered at the Antietam National Battlefield in western Maryland. This battle took place on September 17, 1862, when Confederate General Robert E. Lee tried to invade the North. The fighting at Antietam was extremely fierce. More soldiers were killed or wounded in one day than on any other day of the war. Antietam was the bloodiest battle of the whole war.

The outcome of this battle was probably influenced because a Union soldier found a packet of cigars wrapped in paper. Unbelievably, written on the paper was General Lee's plan to divide his army into five units to attack the Union troops! This important information helped Union General George McClellan halt Lee's invasion of the North. He was able to force the Confederates back to Virginia.

Two Critical Union Victories

At Vicksburg National Military Park, you can relive the horrendous Union attack on the Confederate fort that controlled the Mississippi River. For 47 days, General Grant's cannons pounded Vicksburg. The people caught inside the town had little water or food. They dug caves to escape the shelling. By July 4, 1863, the situation was hopeless, and the city surrendered. The Union now controlled the Mississippi River, slicing the Confederacy in two.

Another Union victory took place the day before Vicksburg fell. This battle in a small village is considered one of the most important of the entire war. It signaled the beginning of the end for the Confederacy. After his troops were beaten there, Robert E. Lee never again invaded the North. At the same time, Grant's army tightened its stranglehold on the South. The name of the small village in Pennsylvania will live forever: Gettysburg.

You honor the memory and importance of this battle when you visit the Gettysburg National Military Park.

You can learn about the bravery of the soldiers by exploring places such as Little Round Top and Cemetery Ridge. You can also follow in the footsteps of the Confederate charge led by General George Pickett. In this battle, 7,000 soldiers were lost. When you visit, be sure to watch the Cyclorama. This is a huge circular painting of Pickett's Charge with a sound-and-light program. Monuments to both sides dot the now-peaceful landscape. Have you ever seen a cyclorama?

Gettysburg battle scene

Stirring Words

If you visit Gettysburg, you can also see where one of the greatest speeches in history was given. The speaker was President Abraham Lincoln. In November 1863, he helped dedicate a cemetery to those who died in the battle. His speech took just two minutes, but it explained why the Union was fighting the war.

In the speech, Lincoln reminded his listeners that their nation was "conceived [created] in Liberty, and dedicated to the proposition [idea] that all men are created equal." He told them that it was beyond his—or anyone's—power to honor the ground in which the soldiers were to be buried. They had already honored it by their deaths. He called their deaths "the last full measure of devotion."

Lincoln ended by challenging his listeners. "Let us highly resolve [decide]," the president said, "that these dead shall not have died in vain—that this nation, under God, shall have a new birth of freedom—and that government of the people, by the people, for the people, shall not perish from the earth." You may have heard those words before. Now you know when, where, and why they were first spoken.

"The War Is Over"

You might also want to visit one other Civil War site. At Appomattox Court House National Historical Park in Virginia, you can stand in Wilmer McLean's home. Why is this house important? Here, on April 9, 1865, the long conflict ended. Two great generals finally met face to face.

Ford's Theatre National Historic Site

General Lee surrendered his ragged army to General Grant. Grant told his men, "The war is over—the Rebels are our countrymen again."

The war that began four years earlier in the choking smoke and flames at Fort Sumter had ended. The healing of the country's wounds was about to begin. Sadly, the man who preserved the Union in its darkest hour never shared in the healing. Abraham Lincoln was murdered at Ford's Theatre two days after the surrender at Appomattox. You can see where the president was shot and where he died if you visit Ford's Theatre National Historic Site in Washington, D.C.

31

CHAPTER 5
A Birthday Present

In New York Harbor stands the world's most famous—and largest—birthday present. It was built to celebrate the hundredth anniversary of American independence.

The year was 1876, and the United States was 100 years old. France had helped the new country win its independence from Great Britain a century before. Now it wanted to help celebrate the hundredth birthday of American freedom. A sculptor named Frédéric-Auguste Bartholdi had an idea.

Sculpting a model of the Statue of Liberty

His birthday present to America would be a statue of a woman. She would be 151 feet (46 m) high and hold the torch of liberty. Her skin would be 300 thin sheets of copper, and she would weigh 225 tons. Her skeleton would be a set of iron braces, designed by engineer Gustave Eiffel. A few years later, he designed and built the famous Eiffel Tower in Paris.

Bartholdi called the bronze woman "Liberty Enlightening the World." Building the statue took eight years. It was done in a workshop in France and was shipped in pieces across the ocean in 214 huge boxes. It took another two years to put the statue back together and build a base for it.

Finally, on October 28, 1886, the statue was finished. Boats filled the harbor, people paraded through New York City, and President Grover Cleveland gave a speech. When Frédéric-Auguste Bartholdi pulled a rope, the huge cloth covering the face of the statue dropped. Cannons boomed, flags waved, and the horns of 300 ships blared. There, for all the world to see, stood the Statue of Liberty.

Including her base, Lady Liberty stands 305 feet (93 m) high. That makes her as tall as a football field is long! Her nose alone extends for 4.5 feet (1.4 m)!

In 1883, Emma Lazarus wrote a famous poem. In her poem, Lady Liberty speaks to other nations of the world. The poem, as the statue, symbolizes America's open arms to people arriving from around the world. Today, the poem is displayed inside the statue's base.

Give me your tired, your poor,
*Your huddled masses **yearning** to breathe free,*
*The **wretched refuse** of your **teeming** shore.*
*Send these, the homeless, the **tempest**-tost, to me*
I lift my lamp beside the golden door.

DID YOU KNOW?
Statue of Liberty

- Climbing from the base to the crown is like walking up a 22-story building.
- The statue's index finger is 8 feet (2.4 m) long.
- The statue was copper-colored, but weather has turned its skin green.
- Ships entering New York Harbor once used the statue's torch as a beacon.
- In 1989, Chinese students were protesting for greater freedom and democracy. They built a version of the Statue of Liberty in Beijing's Tiananmen Square.

The Great Hall at Ellis Island

The Statue of Liberty is one of the most popular national monuments. More than 5.5 million people visited it in the year 2000. Nearby is Ellis Island, part of the Statue of Liberty National Monument. It was the nation's "front door" for many immigrants who came to the United States. More than 12 million immigrants passed through its gates from 1892 to 1954.

Do you have an ancestor who passed through Ellis Island? If you don't know, ask your relatives. You might hear some interesting stories.

At its peak, Ellis Island included 35 buildings, including the Great Hall. In this massive room, as many as 5,000 people a day were processed. Ellis Island is now a fascinating museum. You can see an award-winning film, *Island of Hope, Island of Tears*. The title describes Ellis Island perfectly.

CAN YOU IMAGINE?
The Immigration Process

Can you imagine what it was like to arrive at Ellis Island as a new immigrant? After your ship landed, you would face long hours of waiting in lines. You would be surrounded by a gaggle of strange people. They would be speaking dozens of languages and wearing the clothing of their faraway homelands. As you waited, many questions would run through your mind. Would you be allowed to enter? What would your future hold?

Officials, usually through **interpreters,** would examine your papers. Then doctors would check you for disease. If you had one of many illnesses, you might have to stay for weeks in a crowded dormitory. Then doctors might allow you to enter the United States. Or you might be sent back to your homeland.

If you were accepted, you would have still more questions. How would your life change in this new country? Would you ever see your friends and relatives back home again? All this time, the famous statue would be standing in the harbor just outside the Great Hall. You might wonder if her torch of freedom was lighting the way for you.

CHAPTER 6
WARS IN RECENT TIMES

The opening shots of still another war are honored at one of America's most unusual historic sites. How is it different from most monuments? This one lies under the waters of Pearl Harbor, Hawaii. The USS *Arizona* Memorial honors more than 2,000 sailors and others who lost their lives. They died in America's first battle during World War II. They were killed in a surprise Japanese attack on the U.S. naval base near Honolulu.

"This Is No Drill!"

On the morning of December 7, 1941, U.S. radar operators picked up a large number of incoming planes on their screens. However, they mistook them for American fighters. Less than an hour later, 360 Japanese fighters, bombers, and torpedo planes reached the naval base. Below them sat 92 battleships, destroyers, and other anchored ships of the U.S. Pacific Fleet.

The Japanese planes flew through the morning mist. Then they began to drop their bombs with deadly effect. Within three minutes, this announcement blared through the base's loudspeaker system: "Air raid, Pearl Harbor—This is no drill!" What terror—and anger—the people there must have felt!

The USS **Arizona** *Memorial*

The attack took a dreadful toll. It killed 2,403 Americans and wounded 1,178. Of the 96 ships in port, 18 were sunk or heavily damaged. Fortunately, three of the Pacific Fleet's aircraft carriers were at sea on December 7 and avoided destruction. The attack also destroyed over 200 airplanes.

On the day following the attack, President Franklin Roosevelt asked Congress to declare war against Japan. The surprise raid had forced the United States to enter World War II. The war ended almost four years later. By then, over a million Americans had been killed or wounded. Millions more around the world also lost their lives.

Of the battleships damaged in the attack at Pearl Harbor, all but two were repaired. They later saw action in the war. One that was not repaired was the USS *Arizona*. This battleship has not moved since December 7, 1941. It sits today just below the ocean's surface. Buried inside the ship are the bodies of 1,177 crewmen. They died when the boat caught fire and sank.

Built over the sunken hull of the *Arizona* is a special building. It contains exhibits relating to the attack. One section of the building is called the Shrine Room. On the walls are the names of all the men who went to the bottom with the *Arizona*.

Remembering an Injustice

You can understand why Americans were enraged by the surprise attack on Pearl Harbor. In a short time, the nation was united in the effort to defeat our enemies, Japan and Nazi Germany. However, another historic site demonstrates a dark side of American participation in World War II. It is the Manzanar National Historic Site in eastern California.

On February 19, 1942, President Franklin Roosevelt signed an order that would drastically change the lives of more than 110,000 people. The order affected Japanese Americans, both citizens and legal aliens. It required them to leave their homes and move to "relocation" camps. Why? The United States was at war with Japan. Many Americans feared that people of Japanese ancestry might be a threat to the United States.

Other Americans, however, disagreed strongly with the

39

relocations. They believed that the rights of Japanese Americans were being violated. They pointed out that Americans of German ancestry were not taken from their homes and placed in prison camps.

The region around Manzanar is extremely dry, hot, and dusty in the summer and bitterly cold in the winter. Winds howl off the Sierra Nevada Mountains to the west. The prisoners had to endure a climate very different from the gentler one they were used to.

The Manzanar camp was one of ten camps in the West. It held over 10,000 people as prisoners. They lived in 576 barracks, with entire families squeezed into one room. Barbed-wire fences and armed guards in towers kept the prisoners inside the camp. Today, visitors can see how the prisoners endured their harsh lives. Many of them built rock gardens. At the camp auditorium, they presented plays, concerts, and other kinds of performances.

Manzanar National Historic Site

In time, people realized that a terrible injustice was done to Japanese Americans. The federal government officially apologized in 1988. It offered payments to help make up for the imprisonments. The Manzanar National Historic Site is a harsh reminder of what can happen when racism overrides the law. As you grow older, you can help make sure this kind of injustice does not happen again.

Healing the Scars

Another controversial event in our nation's history is honored at the Vietnam Veterans National Memorial. It is on the Mall in Washington, D.C. Do you know how the Vietnam War began? Near the end of World War II, a civil war started in Vietnam, which is in Southeast Asia. In 1954, the country divided into two parts. A Communist government, supported by the Soviet Union, ruled in North Vietnam. In South Vietnam, the United States and its allies supported another government. At first, the U.S. advised the South Vietnamese army in its battles with the North. After the South Vietnamese suffered setbacks, however, the U.S. began to send American troops to Vietnam.

U.S. soldiers fought in this war from 1963 to 1973. The war bitterly divided Americans. They disagreed over whether it was right or wrong. Some people protested against the war. Others supported the war. They believed that the United States should oppose Communism in every part of the world.

At the peak of the war in April 1969, 543,000 Americans were stationed in Vietnam. As the war

Vietnam Veterans National Memorial

continued, more and more Americans came to believe that the U.S. could not defeat the North Vietnamese army and its ally, the Viet Cong. The United States looked for ways to withdraw from the war. The goal was to leave the fighting to the South Vietnamese army. The last U.S. soldier left Vietnam in March 1973. The South Vietnamese fought on for two more years. However, they were unable to prevent a Communist takeover. All of Vietnam was under Communist control by 1975.

Some American soldiers who returned from the war were bitter. They felt the nation's goals in fighting the war were unclear. Unlike the heroes of earlier wars, Vietnam veterans did not return to parades and celebrations. They were sometimes met with anger from Americans who did not support the war. In 1980, Congress decided to try to change this situation. It authorized a memorial to the men and women who served in the war.

A Controversial Memorial for a Controversial War

A contest was held to design the memorial. The winner was a 21-year-old college senior at Yale University, Maya Ying Lin. She explained that her design was meant to create a peaceful place. It would be a place where people could think about the meaning of the war and its effects on the nation. The memorial consists of two black granite walls that form a "V" rising out of the ground. Each wall is almost 247 feet (75 m) long. After the walls were completed, a bronze statue of three soldiers was added nearby.

In the shiny black surface of the walls are carved the names of more than 58,100 men and women. They all died or are still identified as missing in action. As visitors read the names of the dead and MIAs, they see their own reflections in the shiny stone surface.

Some people felt that the memorial was not fitting. Perhaps they are the ones who did not support the war.

43

Yet many visitors find that the solemn memorial, with its thousands of carved names, is very moving. Letters, photos, flowers, and flags have been placed near the names of loved ones. Over the last twenty years, the "Wall" has become one of the most-visited spots in Washington. A center nearby provides information about the servicemen and women listed on the walls.

Perhaps one of your relatives or some of your classmates' relatives are listed on the walls. Many families were deeply affected by this war.

CHAPTER 7
STRUGGLING FOR JUSTICE

In the previous chapters, you have read about historic places relating to our country's wars. Some national monuments honor another kind of struggle, the struggle for justice. Both kinds of sites preserve our American heritage and teach important lessons. By learning from these sites, we can become better Americans.

Imagining a Different World

In 1848, an American woman's world was a very different place than it is today. Women could not vote. Unmarried women could not attend college, hold office, or even speak out in public on important issues. They could work only as teachers, nurses, maids, waitresses, factory workers, or seamstresses.

At that time, women surrendered most of the rights they had when they got married. They could not own property, sign contracts, or file lawsuits. They could not win custody of their own children. They could not divorce a violent, abusive husband.

On July 19, 1848, about 300 women and men gathered in the village of Seneca Falls. This is in the Finger Lakes region of western New York. They met to discuss women's rights. Their leaders included Elizabeth Cady Stanton and Lucretia Mott.

American Suffragettes, New York City

    The people at this meeting had read Thomas Jefferson's Declaration of Independence. Why, they asked, were women not allowed the "pursuit of life, liberty, and happiness," just like men? Most of these people also condemned the enslavement of African Americans in the Southern states. They believed that the legal and economic slavery of women was just as evil.

    During the meeting, the discussions and debates led to the writing of a Declaration of Sentiments. Echoing the Declaration of Independence, it said, "We hold these truths to be self-evident: that all men *and women* are created equal."

The meeting was called the Women's Rights Convention. The group passed eleven resolutions unanimously. The twelfth one was the most controversial. It said that women should be allowed to vote. Many people at the convention, along with many in the United States, felt this was going too far. They didn't think that women should have the right to vote! The resolution calling for voting rights for women barely passed, thanks to the strong support of Elizabeth Cady Stanton.

When the resolutions passed by the convention became known, many Americans laughed at them. Newspaper editorials around the country made fun of the women. However, the women were not embarrassed. They were determined to continue. The work of this convention became the basis for the continuing progress of political and legal rights for American women. During the rest of the 1800s, Stanton, Mott, and Susan B. Anthony led the battle for changes in the laws.

At first, reform came slowly. In 1860, New York State passed laws giving a married woman some rights. She could own property, keep her wages, file lawsuits, and share custody of her children with her husband after a divorce. In 1869, the territory of Wyoming gave women the right to vote. Then Colorado and Idaho also allowed women to vote.

However, it was not until 1919 that Congress passed the Nineteenth Amendment to the U.S. Constitution. It gave all women the right to vote. A year later, enough states had approved the amendment so that it became law—at last!

Elizabeth Cady Stanton

Mary Ann McClintock home

Other reforms took even longer. In 1963, Congress passed a law requiring equal pay for men and women doing the same federal government jobs. You might be surprised to learn that before this time, women were often paid less for doing exactly the same work as men. That doesn't seem fair today, does it? A civil rights law was passed in 1964 that outlawed discrimination based on sex or race.

Visitors to the Women's Rights National Historical Park can see exhibits about the struggle for women's rights, as well as the convention and its leaders. The homes of two of them, Elizabeth Cady Stanton and Mary Ann McClintock, are included in the park. Visitors can learn how a small group met 150 years ago and planned for equal rights for women.

Liberty and Justice for All

Several historic sites honor the struggle for equal rights for all races. You know that slavery was outlawed at the end of the Civil War. However, did you know that most African Americans did not gain equal rights or opportunities? Many remained in poverty, receiving little or no education. Laws restricted their rights and freedoms. Some brave pioneers spoke out against this inequality. Many worked to correct these conditions.

Meeting With President Lincoln

America's first great African American leader is honored at a national historic site. In Washington, D.C., stands Cedar Hill, a stately white house with a wide front porch. The man who lived in the house wrote, "Do not judge me by the heights to which I have risen, but by the depths from which I have come."

He had been born a slave in Maryland in 1817. He gained his freedom in 1838 when he escaped to the North. His intelligence and passionate opposition to slavery quickly made him a leading **abolitionist,** a person who wants to stop slavery. The man was such a gifted speaker that many people doubted he had ever been a slave. Do you know who this man was?

The man published his autobiography in 1845. *Life and Times of Frederick Douglass* became a bestseller. Frederick Douglass met with President Lincoln often during the Civil War. He helped convince the president that African Americans should be allowed to fight in the Union Army.

From 1877 until his death in 1895, Cedar Hill was Douglass's home. It was also a center for the causes he strongly supported. You can visit Cedar Hill today and learn about the amazing life and career of Douglass.

Up from Slavery

Another African American leader is honored at the Booker T. Washington National Monument and the Tuskegee Institute National Historic Site. Like Douglass, Washington was born a slave but became an outstanding African American leader during the last half of the 1800s. Tuskegee Institute is the school that he founded in Alabama.

Frederick Douglass

Booker T. Washington was born in 1856 in Virginia. His owner estimated his value at $400. Can you imagine having a price attached to you? His family gained their freedom following the Civil War and moved to West Virginia. There the young boy found work in a coal mine and a salt factory.

However, Washington was determined to go to school. He became a student at Hampton Institute in Virginia, a school for African Americans. Working as a janitor as he studied, Washington graduated in 1875. Then he became a schoolteacher.

In 1881, he was asked to head a new school for African Americans in Tuskegee, Alabama. The school started with almost no money and two neglected buildings. Would you like to attend a school like that? Washington built the school into a university with 1,500 students and more than 100 buildings.

Washington became convinced that African Americans should learn farming and industrial skills. These skills would help them gain economic security. Then, he believed, political equality would come over time.

In his autobiography, *Up from Slavery,* Washington described how his views developed from his own experiences. What lessons do you think young people—and adults—can learn at the Booker T. Washington National Monument about this man?

There are two historic sites where you can learn how the nation's schools and other public places became **integrated,** or open to people of all races. At one time, schools in the United States were **segregated**. There were schools for black students and schools for white students.

In 1896, the Supreme Court of the United States ruled that public facilities, such as railroad cars, could be segregated by race. The two facilities just had to be "equal." The ruling was later used to support school segregation. However, you will not be surprised to learn

Anti-segregation protest, Missouri, 1963

that in many states, schools for white children were much better than schools for black children.

In 1951, a third grader named Linda Brown lived in Topeka, Kansas. Her home was near an elementary school. However, she had to walk a half-mile to a bus stop and then ride two more miles to another school. Why? She was an African American, and the nearby school was for white children only. Her parents sued the city school board. They wanted their daughter to be able to attend the nearby school.

Over the next three years, several courts heard the lawsuit, called *Brown* v. *Board of Education of Topeka*. Finally, the lawsuit reached the Supreme Court. This court's decision would become the law of the land. Do you know how the court ruled?

On May 17, 1954, the Supreme Court announced its fateful decision. "Separate but equal" schools, it said, were nearly always unequal. After the ruling, segregation in schools was illegal. This was one of the first great victories for the civil rights movement. Today, Linda's school, Monroe Elementary, is the Brown v. Board of Education National Historic Site.

Three years after the historic court decision, nine African American students tried to enroll at Little Rock Central High School in the Arkansas capital. The governor of the state refused to allow the students to register. He ordered the state's national guard to prevent the students from entering the school. Crowds of angry white students and adults shouted insults and threats at the students. Can you imagine how the nine African American students felt? What would you have done if you were in their place?

President Dwight Eisenhower sent federal troops to protect the black students. They were allowed to enroll at the school, and the desegregation of other Southern schools followed. Little Rock Central High School is now a national historic site. It honors the courage of the African American students.

Students escorted into school, Little Rock, Arkansas

"I Have a Dream"

In Atlanta, Georgia, you can explore the life of Martin Luther King, Jr. You can see where he was born, lived, and worked. You can also visit his grave. The Martin Luther King, Jr., National Historic Site includes his childhood home. It also includes the Ebenezer Baptist Church, where King served as pastor.

Throughout the 1950s and 1960s, King led the struggle for civil rights. In 1955, he led a **boycott** of the bus system in Montgomery, Alabama. By refusing to ride the buses, African Americans forced the city to integrate them. King's belief in nonviolence gained him many admirers. In 1964, he won the Nobel Prize for peace for his campaign for equal rights.

    King also led one of the most famous rallies in United States history. It was the March on Washington on August 28, 1963. The date was chosen to honor the hundredth anniversary of Abraham Lincoln's Emancipation Proclamation, which had freed slaves in many Southern states. On this day, more than 200,000 people of all races

Martin Luther King, Jr.

heard the young preacher and civil rights leader speak. His speech that day has become as well known as those of Abraham Lincoln.

Martin Luther King, Jr., stood in front of the statue of the Great Emancipator. "I have a dream," he announced, "that my four little children will one day live in a nation where they will not be judged by the color of their skin, but by the content of their character." He looked forward to the day when all people would "be able to join hands and sing in the words of the old Negro spiritual, 'Free at last! Free at last! Thank God Almighty, we are free at last!'"

Some people feared King's ideas. He was assassinated in Memphis, Tennessee, in 1968. The Martin Luther King, Jr., National Historic Site honors his dream of making America a place where all people can "sit down together at the table of brotherhood."

CHAPTER 8
CELEBRATING AMERICA'S GREATNESS

Not all of our country's national monuments honor wars or struggles for equality. Can you think of other important events that have shaped America's history? How about scientific discoveries, the growth of industry, and the search for new territories and a new way of life?

The First Flight

Picture in your mind a place where the age of flight might begin. What would it look like? In fact, few places on Earth look *less* like a modern airport than the place where flight began. It is a wind swept beach on the North Carolina coast. It's far from any big city. There are no runways in sight. Instead of the roar of jumbo jets, the only sound is the crash of the surf. However, a hundred years ago, this stretch of beach witnessed something never before seen.

How did this happen? Here is what Wilbur Wright wrote in 1900:

"For some years I have been afflicted with the belief that flight is possible to man. . . .I have been trying to arrange my affairs in such a way that I can devote my entire time . . . to experiment."

The Wright brothers and their bicycle shop in Dayton, Ohio

The bicycle shop that Wilbur operated in Dayton, Ohio, with his brother Orville was doing a good business. Still, the brothers took off more and more time for their study of flight. They studied others' experiments. They watched birds for hours to see how their wings lifted them into the sky. The brothers built models, kites, and gliders. They were interested in anything that would help them unlock the secret of flight.

In 1900, the Wrights traveled to Kitty Hawk, North Carolina. It was a great place to test their ideas about the construction of a flying machine. There, they began to test a glider that was 17 feet (5.2 m) long. Although the glider had problems staying in the air, the Wrights were encouraged.

They returned to Dayton and continued to tinker with the machine's design. Their next glider had an even wider wingspan and more of a curve along the top of the wing. The design was still not satisfactory, however. When they tested the glider at Kitty Hawk, it was hard to control. Still, the brothers did not give up.

Back to the Drawing Board!

The Wrights' next design included an upright tail that helped keep the glider steady. After almost 400 tests and more tinkering, Orville decided to make the tail movable. He also connected it with the movable parts of the wings. Another 600 test glides gave the brothers confidence that they were very close to flying. In 1903, they built a small, lightweight gasoline engine. The engine would power two small propellers mounted in the center of the plane, facing backwards. The pilot would lie on his stomach in the middle of the plane. That would take courage, don't you think?

Finally, they returned to Kill Devil Hill, a small hill near Kitty Hawk. The brothers attached the engine to a new glider named the *Flyer*. They made improvements to their aircraft. By December, they were ready for the big test. On December 14, Wilbur piloted the *Flyer* but crashed it into the sand. They repaired it and tried again three days

A replica of the **Flyer** *at Wright Brothers National Memorial*

later. This time Orville was at the controls. As Wilbur ran alongside, Orville flew the plane for 120 feet (37 m) and 12 seconds. When he landed the plane gently on the sand, the brothers had done what nobody had before.

They made three more successful flights that day. The last one covered 850 feet (259 m) and lasted for almost a minute. Then a gust of wind flipped the *Flyer* over. It would never fly again, but it was still the first flying machine.

You can see a replica of it at Wright Brothers National Memorial. Be sure to check out the other exhibits, too. You can learn more about the courage and dedication of the two Ohio bicycle makers. They showed that people could, indeed, fly like birds.

North to Alaska

In 1896, three explorers of a different kind made a discovery while roaming near the Klondike River in northwestern Canada. They saw shiny yellow pebbles glinting in the clear waters of Bonanza Creek. Could it be?

The men's greatest hopes proved true. When word of their discovery reached Seattle, the rush was on. In the summer of 1898, newspaper headlines screamed "Gold Discovered in the Klondike!"

The Klondike Gold Rush started a stampede. Many hopeful prospectors began their journeys in Seattle. From there, they took a boat to Skagway, on Alaska's coast just north of Juneau. The boat trip was the easy part. From Skagway, they had to hike over mountains. Often they

Klondike gold mining town, Klondike, Yukon Territory

were lugging hundreds of pounds of equipment. The sudden arrival of 30,000 rough-and-ready gold hunters turned sleepy Alaskan towns into rowdy zoos!

As it turned out, few of these prospectors hit pay dirt. Some died on the dangerous overland trail to the Klondike gold fields. They became victims of the treacherous weather, steep slopes, or hungry bears and wolves. Most turned around and went home. They ended up rich in experience but not in gold. The Klondike Territory turned out to contain many other valuable minerals but not much gold. The territory has become an important source of silver, lead, zinc, copper, coal, and iron. It also has some petroleum and natural gas.

Would you like to relive these exciting days? You can—by visiting the Klondike Gold Rush National Historical Park. Part of the park is in the Pioneer Square Historic District in Seattle. Here, many people first heard about the yellow pebbles in the faraway Klondike. Other parts of the park are in Skagway and along the trail over the rugged mountains. Among the buildings you can see in Skagway are the railroad depot, a historic saloon, and miners' cabins.

Where It All Began

The Klondike gold fields offered the hope of quick riches. However, you can visit several memorials that represent America's *true* path to wealth. Unlike the Klondike, these sites explain the reasons for our country's real rise to power. They are dedicated to the beginning of the Industrial Revolution in America.

As early as 1646, 26 years after the Pilgrims landed at Plymouth Rock, people in America needed iron. Iron is a heavy, hard metal, one of the most common on Earth. After it is mined, it undergoes smelting. During this process, the iron ore is heated to a high temperature to purify it and remove other materials. Then it is formed into useful shapes. If the chair you are sitting in has steel legs, they were made from iron.

The Pilgrims used iron to make nails, hinges, tools, kettles, pots, pans, and many other items. John Winthrop, Jr., was the son of the governor of the Massachusetts Bay Colony. He decided to build an integrated iron works. In an integrated works, all the steps in creating a product are performed at one location. It's a "one-stop shop."

Winthrop built his iron works a few miles north of Boston in the village of Saugus. By 1650, it was one of the most advanced iron works in the world. Winthrop had recruited experienced ironworkers from

Saugus Iron Works National Historic Site

England and Scotland. The workers and their families lived in a small town Winthrop had built. Wherever they went in town, residents could see the glow from the furnaces. They could hear the heavy hammers pounding the iron into shapes. The iron works operated around the clock for almost 30 years.

Visitors to the Saugus Iron Works National Historic Site today can see how the iron was smelted, transported, and shaped. They can see how the workers and their families lived. They can trace our country's industrial power back to its humble beginnings.

Near Saugus is the Lowell National Historical Park. It marks the true beginning of large-scale manufacturing in the United States. There you can tour the first large factory in America, the Lowell Cotton Mill. The park also contains exhibits showing how the United States changed from a farming economy to an industrial one. It will help you learn more about industrial technology and the roles that immigrants played in the rise of America's factories.

How did the Lowell Cotton Mill come about? In the early 1800s, a businessman named Francis Lowell decided to build a textile mill just outside of Boston. He knew that the rushing water of the Merrimack River could power the mill's machinery. Within a few years, he had completed the world's first modern textile factory. In it, machines carded (cleaned and combed) raw cotton, spun it into thread, and then wove it into cloth.

Many of the workers in Lowell's factory were young girls. They had left their families' farms to work for much higher wages in the new mill. Life changed greatly for the workers in Lowell's factory. Many lived in company-owned dormitories. Although Lowell's workers were treated well, other factories were dusty, dirty, and dangerous. No doubt, many mill workers wished they were back home on their farms.

Exhibits at the park will help you understand what the workers' lives were like. You can learn about their goals and dreams back then. Do you think they were much like your own?

You can also trace the developments in technology that led to the rise of America's industrial might. Our industries are the true source of our nation's wealth.

Lowell National Historical Park

CHAPTER 9
Fire and Water

People living in southwestern Washington State had gotten used to seeing the gorgeous, snow-capped mountain on the horizon. Mount Saint Helens is part of the Cascade Range. The Cascades divide the states of Washington and Oregon. The quiet forests, crystal-clear lakes, and breathtaking scenery around the mountain made it a popular spot. Many people went there to camp, hike, fish, and picnic. Then one event changed everything.

In the spring of 1980, people began to notice strange signs near the mountain. They saw puffs of steam and ash in the sky. They felt small earthquakes. They asked each other what might be happening. Can you guess what was going to occur? On the morning of May 18, the top of Mount Saint Helens exploded. The volcano had awakened!

The explosion of the erupting volcano could be heard 200 miles (320 km) away. Clouds of ash, smoke, and hot gases reached more than 12 miles (20 km) into the air. A frightening avalanche of rock, hot mud, and ash roared down the mountainside. It instantly buried everything in its path. The avalanche sped down the mountain slopes at up to 155 miles (250 km) an hour!

Erupting Mount Saint Helens

The flows spread as far as 17 miles (27 km) away from the mountain. Sixty-two people and thousands of animals were killed. More than six million trees were destroyed. Thick gray ash covered cars, homes, and even pets up to 930 miles (1,500 km) away. Can you imagine how that looked?

When the smoke cleared, people were shocked to see what had happened to Mount Saint Helens. The snow-capped peak was completely gone. In its place was a horseshoe-shaped crater. The rim of the crater was about 8,000 feet (2,400 m) high. As time passed, the rim filled with water, forming a clear volcanic lake.

Mount Saint Helens is peaceful now. At the Mount Saint Helens National Volcanic Monument, you can learn about the awesome eruption. It was one of the largest ever recorded in North America. You can see items burned by the smoke and ash. Some had been buried in the flow of mud and debris. You can examine photos taken by **volcanologists**. These scientists study volcanoes. Most of all, you can experience the incredible power of one of nature's mightiest creations.

DID YOU KNOW?
Volcanoes

- Clouds often form above erupting volcanoes and produce lightning.
- Volcanoes at the bottom of the ocean erupt continuously, spreading lava over the sea bottom.
- Earthquakes often trigger volcanic eruptions. An earthquake measuring 5.1 on the Richter scale occurred early on May 18, 1980, at Mount Saint Helens.
- Other famous volcanoes are Vesuvius in Italy, Mauna Loa in Hawaii, Kilimanjaro in Tanzania, Paracutín in Mexico, Fuji in Japan, and Krakatoa in Indonesia.
- The word *volcano* comes from Vulcan, the ancient Roman god of fire and blacksmithing.

A Deadly Wall of Water

A national memorial in central Pennsylvania honors another kind of natural disaster. It took many more lives than the eruption of Mount Saint Helens.

The disaster began as heavy rains fell on the night of May 30, 1889. Many people in Johnstown, Pennsylvania, began to worry about the South Fork Dam. This dam was high in the mountains, ten miles northeast of the city. It had been built of packed earth, creating a **reservoir** of water. The next afternoon, as the rain continued, the dam began to crumble. Suddenly, the dam broke.

Flood damage in Johnstown, Pennsylvania

A deadly wall of water, 30 feet (10 m) high, raced down the mountain towards the city. The floodwaters reached speeds of 40 miles (64 km) an hour. At 4:07 P.M., 20 million tons of water struck the town with terrifying force. Can you imagine the panic of the people in its path? Within minutes, most of the northern half of the city was in ruins. More than 2,200 people were killed. About 1,600 homes were destroyed. This was by far the deadliest flood in U.S. history.

Today, you can visit the Johnstown Flood National Memorial. You can see the place high in the mountains where the dam gave way. Down in the city of Johnstown, be sure to visit Grandview Cemetery. Here lie more than 700 victims of this spectacular disaster. They have never been identified.

Now you know more about America's monuments that honor special times and events. They include forts and battlefields, huge statues and small churches, meeting places and old factories. When you visit these national monuments, you learn about the events that shaped our country. You learn how the past led to our great and free nation.

Which of the monuments would you like to visit? Which recent events do you think qualify to become new national monuments?

INTERESTING FACTS ABOUT OUR NATIONAL MONUMENTS

- New national monuments and memorials are being created today. For example, the Oklahoma City National Memorial honors the 168 people who died in the 1995 terrorist bombing. It became a memorial in 1997.
- The national monuments and other special places in this book are under the control of the U.S. National Park Service. The National Park Service is a part of the Department of the Interior. The federal taxes we all pay help the National Park Service preserve and protect our nation's special places.

Bibliography

Butcher, Devereux. *Exploring Our National Parks and Monuments,* 9th edition. Niwot, CO: Roberts Rinehart Publishers, 1995.

Butcher, Russell. *Exploring Our National Historic Parks and Sites.* Niwot, CO: Roberts Rinehart Publishers, 1997.

Reader's Digest. *America's Historic Places: An Illustrated Guide to Our Country's Past.* Pleasantville, NY: The Reader's Digest Association, 1988.

Van Rose, Susanna. *Volcano and Earthquake: an Eyewitness Book.* New York: DK Publishing, 2000.

You can also find more information about our national monuments at these Web sites:

www.gorp.com
   a site devoted to outdoor adventures

www.nps.gov
   the National Park Services ParkNet page; information about parks, monuments, memorials, and other NPS sites

Web sites have been carefully researched for accuracy, content, and appropriateness. However, Web sites are subject to change. Internet usage should always be monitored.

Glossary

abolitionist (ab•uh•**li**•shuhn•ist) person opposed to slavery

barracks (**bar**•uhks) buildings to house soldiers or prisoners

barricades (**bar**•i•kaydz) walls to stop movement

boycott (**boy**•kot) refusal to use or take part in something

civilians (si•**vil**•yuhnz) people not in the armed services

integrated (**in**•ti•gray•tid) open to people of all races

interpreters (in•**tur**•pri•tuhrz) persons who translate from one language to another

refuse (**ref**•yoos) something that is thrown away

reservoir (**rez**•uhr•vwar) pond or lake used to store water

secede (si•**seed**) to withdraw

segregated (**seg**•ri•gay•tid) separated by races

teeming (**teem**•ing) crowded

tempest (**tem**•pist) storm

treaty (**tree**•tee) agreement

volcanologists (vol•kuh•**nol**•uh•jists) scientists who study volcanoes

wretched (**rech**•id) miserable

yearning (**yur**•ning) wishing for

73

INDEX

Antietam National Battlefield 27
Appomattox Court House National Historical Park 30
Bartholdi, Frédéric-Auguste 32–33
Booker T. Washington National Monument 50–51
Borglum, Gutzon 6–10
Brown v. *Board of Education* National Historic Site 53
Civil War 3, 22–31, 49–50
Colonial National Historical Park 15
Douglass, Frederick 49–50
Eiffel, Gustave 33
Ellis Island 35–36
Ford's Theatre National Historic Site 31
Fort Clatsop National Monument 18–19
Fort McHenry National Monument 20–21
Fort Sumter 23, 24, 31
Gateway Arch 17
Gettysburg National Military Park 1, 29–30
Jefferson National Expansion Memorial 16–18
Jefferson, Thomas 1, 6–7, 10, 16–17, 46
Johnstown Flood National Memorial 70–71
Key, Francis Scott 20–21
King, Martin Luther, Jr. 54–56
Klondike Gold Rush National Historical Park 61–62
Lazarus, Emma 33
Lewis and Clark 17–20
Lincoln, Abraham 1, 6–7, 10, 22–23, 30–31, 49, 55–56

Little Rock Central High School	53–54
Lowell National Historical Park	64–65
Manassas	25–26
Manzanar National Historic Site	39–41
Martin Luther King, Jr., National Historic Site	54, 56
Minute Man National Historical Park	11
Mount Rushmore National Monument	6–10
Mount Saint Helens National Volcanic Monument	66–68
Revolutionary War	11–16
Roosevelt, Franklin	38–39
Roosevelt, Theodore	6–7, 10
Saratoga National Historical Park	13–14
Saugus Iron Works National Historic Site	63–64
Shiloh National Military Park	26–27
"The Star-Spangled Banner"	21
Statue of Liberty National Monument	1, 32–35
Tuskegee Institute National Historic Site	50–51
USS *Arizona* Memorial	37–39
Valley Forge National Historical Park	12
Vicksburg National Military Park	28
Vietnam Veterans National Memorial	41–44
War of 1812	20–21
Washington, George	1–2, 6–7, 10, 12, 14
Women's Rights	45–47
World War II	4, 37–40
Wright Brothers National Memorial	57–60
Yorktown	15